# TATVAMAYI

## CONTEMPORARY ISSUES IN MANAGEMENT AND ECONOMICS

BRAJESH KUMAR PANDEY

ISBN 979-888503087-8

*I dedicate this Book to my Late Grandfather Pandit Suryadev Pandey who from the beginning of my life Instilled spiritual faith and Vedic wisdom within me. It was not possible to be what I am today without his guidance and Inspiration.*

*And to mother Durga, to whom I was introduced by my Late Grandfather at mere age of 4 from where on I got devoted to her and today I consider her as my First Mother.*

*And Last but not least to Lord Krishna, my Lord, my Guru and my Everything.*

# Contents

# Preface

*Many of you dream of Studying at top universities of the world like Harvard Stanford and so on, to the extent, apart from those classroom and bookish learning it gives you geographical exposure and peer to peer learning, but nature is the best teacher. Management is not about learning theories in the classroom but practicing it. Time management is what the west is good at, as thought by many of you who have studied abroad, but to tell you the fact, as an astrologer and being closely associated with temples in the Country, nowhere in the world you will learn the importance of time management than in the temples of India, unfortunately we Indians have not followed and practiced it.*

*The purpose of writing this book was to solve many of the worlds current problems and that's possible only through management, even best of economies fails due to poor management. The spine of every economies stands on proper management.*

*I have made a small effort on those topics of management and economies, its my view hope you would like it. This book would be useful for every management students and aspiring entrepreneur who wants to prosper further in life.*

*Brajesh Kumar Pandey*
*Bediban Madhuban*
*East Champaran, Bihar, India-845416*
*Email- tatvamayi@gmail.com*

CHAPTER I

# Role of continuity in Innovation

*A virtuous deed performed again and again makes a person wiser. Growing wiser, a man always performs virtuous deeds. Such a person transcend to heaven.*

*-Vidur*

*There is a English proverb which says Practice makes a man perfect, so does lord Krishna says to Arjun in Bhagwat Gita to Control his sense organs and obtain knowledge and devotion through the yoga of repeated practice. We cannot obtain perfection or mastery in any field without practice and that's not possible without continuity.*

*There is a biological reason for the need of continuity and practice. Our cells in the body keeps on regenerating and vanishes at a certain period of time, hence if we lack continuity as soon as the cells vanishes and new cells comes in we forget many of our thoughts so we need to have continuity in order to have those thoughts and memories in our mind and above it in order to obtain mastery of the subject.*

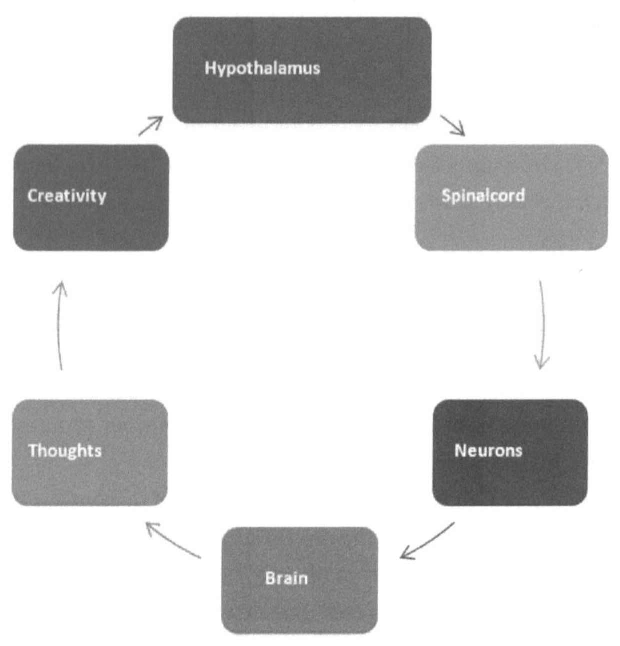


*Genesis of thought process and Ideas*

***Hypothalamus**: hypothalamus has origination from endocrine gland which plays major role in the nature and quality of thoughts coming to our brain through the sensory roots of spinal cord. It's located near to the pituitary gland and has close connection with the spinal cord. The endocrine gland affects a lot in functions of brain and memory. Disorder in thalamus causes thyroid problem and causes memory loss. Hence in order to have a sharp memory we need to have a very sound endocrine gland. It not only helps us in memory* *functions but also the quality of our thoughts which determines the quality of innovation.*

**Spinal cord**:-*sensory root carries to the brain from different parts of the body. The spines plays major role in the brain functions and our vibes. It's the spinal cord which is responsible for the vibes flowing out of our body, because the sensory roots stimulates the thoughts process and sends signals to brain the brain intercepts the feelings and responds back the emotions which is transcended through the spinal cord.*

**Neurons**:-*Neurons are surrounded by many supportive cells from which sheath are formed. The sheath includes a fatty molecule called myelin which provides insulation for the axon and helps nerve signal travel faster and farther. The signal from one cell to another is transferred through neurons.*

**Brain**:- *Thoughts depends up on mind and mind functions as per the signal of brain. And functions of brain mostly depend up on the spinal cord which transmits the signal from the various parts of the body to brain. A repeated practice takes little effort because those thoughts and process are already present in the brain cells or neurons.*

*Grey matter in brain is responsible for creativity which is indirectly connected with spinal cord through the neurons.*

**Thought**: *The thoughts in the brain come from the sense organs of the body transmitted by spinal cord. The quality of thoughts and memory depends up on the quality of endocrine gland which is associated with the hypothalamus. A sound and healthy endocrine will always lead to a healthy thought leading to a healthy mind. Since the cells of all this keeps on regenerating we need continuity in innovative process to have innovative ideas.*

**Creativity**: *Creativity originates from a thought process and is dependent on the above parts and functions of brains.*

*We need to have a good level of curiosity to submerge ourselves in the thought process which leads to creativity. We analyse on the thoughts which regenerate new thoughts many a times these new thoughts gives birth to new ideas and working on this new ideas paves way for creativity.*

*Role Of Discipline in Innovation*

*Innovation in the byproduct of our thought process. since our mind is of wandering nature we need to have control of our mind regarding what we think and that requires a sincere practice. we cannot practice or continue a set of practice without discipline. Thus discipline plays a big role in continuity. Discipline let us to be sincere which and fo the laid path with continuity to lead us to a innovative path. Biologically when we practice the same set of rules a on daily basis our brain becomes more aware and the autonomic nervous system works much better which is responsible for the signaling to various parts of the body. Its said in yoga that the lower you breathe the more you are aware of nature, the higher is your consciousness level and you understand the activities of nature very well. That require a set of practice and practice requires discipline so indirectly discipline takes you on the path of practice which increases the autonomic nervous system functions. The grey matter in the brain increases with a regular set of practice. It increases the understanding capabilities. When we practice the same thing on regular basis we get in-depth of knowledge about it. The more the knowledge we have of anything, the more we can analyze things Practice increase our curiosity and analytical thinking. Gaining knowledge requires practice and practice requires discipline.*

*so continuity has a lot to do with innovation*

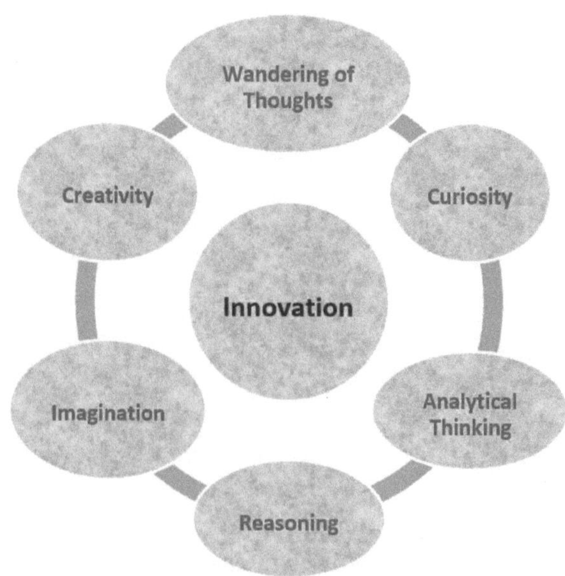


*Innovation is creating something new from the existing circumstances. It can be in a product a service or anything.*

*Innovation depends on two thing creativity and discipline. Both require continuity. Creativity comes from thoughts. Thoughts come from the surrounding. Thoughts process happens in the mind. Mind has a wandering tendencies and it's a fact that without letting our mind wander our thought process get restricted which doesn't let new ideas to come to your mind.*

*Mind has a inherent wandering tendencies and we need to let it wander on a specific areas on which we need to innovate. Our thoughts at a time should be wandering on that specific areas in which we want to procreate. To do this we need our mind should be disciplined.*

*Its true in this thought process many secondary ideas would come which might be not beneficial for that specific product or process , but it might be helpful for some other process which can be saved and carried forward .*

***Wandering of Mind**: in astrology moon is responsible for our thoughts and it's the fastest moving planets, hence our thoughts keep wandering and changing frequently. if we restrict our thoughts it has a tendency it keeps on pondering over that very thoughts, so it's advisable to let our thoughts wander so that fresh thoughts comes to our mind. Unless we let the old one go out the new thoughts will never come in , so let the process continue and you will find your mind filled with abundance of thoughts.*

**Curiosity:-***When thoughts comes to our mind our curiosity get enhanced and so does the thought process .Curiosity gives birth to many new thoughts and there starts analytical thinking. Its curiosity which propels us to question about the thoughts coming into our mind.*

***Analytical thinking**:-Curiosity is the origin of analytical thinking. In analysis we over to ponder over various thoughts in the mind its pros and cons and which one is relevant for us. These set of questionnaire gives birth to reasoning.*

***Reasoning**: As consequence of analytical thinking we start finding the reason for the genesis of the thoughts prevalent at the very moment in to our mind. Mind has the tendency to find the reason for any matter so long as we have curiosity in us alive.*

***Imagination**: - William words worth has said imagination is not but the absolute power. Imagination plays the utmost important role in creativity. So long as we imagine over the thoughts prevalent in our mind we cannot procreate a new ideas. In imagination all the above process significant role. Every poetic verse are the byproduct of imagination. So we* *have to develop imaginative skills by creating images of the thoughts coming in to our mind.*

**Creativity**: *Imagination gives birth to creativity and is directly proportional to curiosity. The more the curiosity the more is the thoughts process in our mind and more frequent is the imagination and greater is the creativity level in our mind.*

*Discipline leads to innovation ,you know mind is of*

*wandering nature and various types of thoughts keep on coming in to our mind, so to let only innovative and positive thoughts come in to our mind we need continuity .Innovation requires a great deal of continuity , continuity requires discipline so they both go hand in hand. By now it should be clear to you all that to maintain and master the body's physiological activities responsible for innovation one need a great deal of continuity. Continuity requires practice. and practice require discipline. So continuity and practice are interdependent on each other and one need to be disciplined in order to be a innovator.*

CHAPTER II

# Behavioral approaches to decision making

*A person who uses harsh words and unbecoming words , who is hot tempered , who hurts others in their weak moments and who pierces others with poisouness barbs is like a pauper or like dregs in a rubbish heap. He carries penury and death in his mouth.*

*-Vidur*

*Behaviour is our communication to different creatures in the nature .it may be human being , birds animals or any living creatures present in the surrounding. Behavior cannot be possible without communication. It's the root of behavior.*

*The curiosity here arises does communication happens only through our tongue, perhaps not, communication happens through our vibes , sign language facial expression and all these constitute to behaviour. It also depends up on our facial expressions, emotion, love , affection, generosity and many more elements.*

*All the above elements are the byproduct of our mind, which is heavily affected by happenings in the surrounding . thus behavior to a large extent depends up on the external environment of the society .*

*Since behavior depends up on the nature of people we are interacting with, hence it depends whole lot on the attitude of the party in the communication.*

*Behavior is a reciprocal phenomenon and it depends a lot on matter and facts in the communication apart from party in the communication. An argumentative communication can lead to change in behavior on the other hand an agreeable communication will always have a better behaviour. It all depends up on the attitude of the party in the communication and matter of facts.*

*Verbal communication is only the least elements of behavior .what matter most in behaviour is our vibes and emotions .the various emotional elements such as expression ,our vibes , love affection etc.. synergies the behavior. The emotional expression in communication reflects the reality of behavior whether its real or articulated. Your speeches would consists of some fascinating and gorgeous words but unless it matches with your expression our behavior would be exposed accordingly.*

*There is biological phenomenon regarding this when our words doesn't associate with our expression our subconscious mind contradicts it and our behavior gets exposed. Hence the subconscious mind contradicts the fake emotions and it getreflacted through various human emotions.*

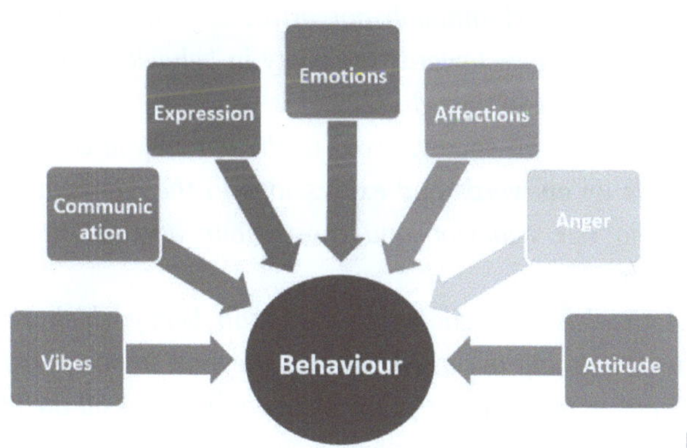

***Vibes**are the flow of thoughts through pranic energy. Perhaps it plays a larger role than the verbal communication. Words can be articulated but not the vibes.*

***Comminication**:it's the verbal communication during our behavior. Here words matters .behavior depends up on Words expressed in the form of communication. Verbal communication is the least factor which influences behavior.*

***Expression**expression-Our behavior is mostly affected by our expression. Unless one is a master crook, no one can fake expression because its directly influenced by subconscious mind. That comes out naturally depending up on the Authenticity of the matter and situation. One should take extreme care of their expression while interaction.*

***Emotion**is connected with our subconscious mind and it's a natural trait of human being. The level of emotion Varies with people to people. Our emotion in behavior depends up the reciprocal conversation and counteractive response from each side. it depends up on the words, expression and off course the vibes **Affection**though not attraction but somewhat an inclination of love towards the party in behavior. it enhances the atmosphere in the behavior.*

***Anger**:-Its an enemy, avoid to the extent you can. Anger depends up on words and expressions in the communication affecting our behavior and mostly our attitude. It spoils behavior.*

***Attitude**is that quality in a human being which is and influenced by our nature. Attitude is the most important factor which plays a major role in the behavior, Perhaps all the above traits are indirectly influenced by our attitude. it's the attitude on which the reciprocal communication depends. Even our vibes depends up on our attitude which affects the behavior to a large extent.*

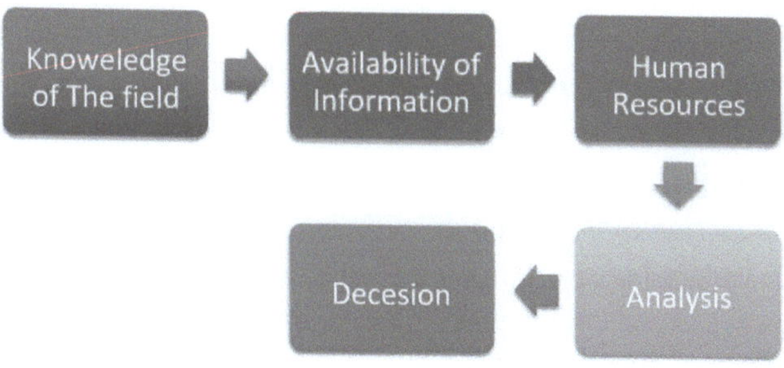


***Knowledge of the field**: one can't make any decision if he has no knowledge about the concerned field. Knowledge does not merely constitute of information available in the text. As a manager or CEO you have to deal with vivid circumstances and you have to take decision according to the situation hence you should have the knowledge involved in various circumstances and situation.*

***Availability of Information**:- decision making is a situation and circumstantial based quality. one need to have All the information of the current situation and other similar circumstances to arrive at any conclusion. Some times while making decision we have to we keep in our mind the previous outcome of the similar circumstance that could be gained through knowledge and practice. Those are also supportive information which helps in decision making*

***Human Resources**:- management is an art and not science, why i say this because in your company various machines work on set of principles, your organization runs on set of principle but decision making doesn't run on any principle. It largely depends upon situation and you need* *master the art to take appropriate decision under vivid circumstances. The quality of human resource to large extent decide the decision making process of an organisation. When i speak of quality of human resource, I mean their knowledge and experience of dealing with various circumstances.*

**Analysis:**-*its performed by human resources of the organization after thorough analysis of available information and knowledge. we can't analyze anything without having knowledge and information. It's on this two thing on which analysis depends. A CEO and manager should have a good analytical mind since business runs on decision making capabilities*

**Decision:**- *after thorough analysis of information and knowledge by the concerned human resource one arrives at decision.*

*Decision making is dependent on situation and in most of the situation human resource are involved, while dealing with human resource behavior plays a major role. Some time we have to keep in our mind the various traits of human being before taking any decision. if one doesn't care about the emotions and feeling of their employees which are there human resources than that will lead to a negative environment in the office . Some time we have to break the barrier and go beyond that to take a decision that might not hurt the sentiments of employees such practices instills faith in the employees. Thus decision making depends a lot on the behavior and various behavioral traits of human being.*

CHAPTER III

# Corporate suicides and a way through out

*Vedic scriptures says aham brahmasmi which means we all are the children of God. And Vedas goes on to the extent saying we can become God. Now that we can become God in our life time why couldn't we understand the importance of our life. Does money makes one God , you are at least that wise to answer that simply no; Had it been than the world richest would pay few billions in temples or churches and would become God. Than why do we give up so easily when we lose just one Goal, one Corporate target, Some few millions of debts.*

*Is Life that Useless? Valueless?*

*If not than Why Suicide?*

*Every human being takes birth on this earth with an intent to perform action according to the three modes of nature inherited from previous birth and one has to exhaust all his karma (action) by performing such action according to the attitude influenced by the three modes of nature which keeps on changing at an regular interval of time by the nature of his action prevailing at that very moment.*

*Corporate suicides is on upsurge not only in our country but worldwide and the sole reason for it are our change in living habits which has failed many of us in coping up with failures and peer pressure which causes stress and leads us to depression and many other newly invented mental diseases which perhaps doesn't exist and on the contrary it causes more mental problems and it compels the victim to feel that he is not in good state of mind which is more than a mental problems. The side effects of the prescribed pills add more woes to his health than curing his mental problems. Since many corporate leaders would be the head of their family , it add woes to their family members that the head of the family his suffering from mental problems and that pressure in return add to the woes to the leader suffering from depression*

*Lets look at the reason of Stress which causes depression which leads to suicidal tendencies*

*Peer Pressure: Human being has some inherent emotions in each one of us such as , love, anger, affection, Empathy , jealousy, comparison etc... and it keeps on altering as per the three modes of nature depending up on the action performed by us at that particular time. when we start comparing our performance with our peers and our neighbors , if our performance are below them we land into low self-esteem at this stage, the law of inertia infatuates our vision. We over think over it and put our brain in to stress . Stress consumes most of our body energy and we feel fatigue. Low self esteem and over stress causes depression and loneliness and some times we think unethical measures to overtake our peers , when we fail in all this, there starts the suicidal tendencies.*

*corporate Target: In this competitive world , CEOs and many managers have a stiff target to fulfill and they are always in a thinking process to find a measures to fulfill its sales goals. They feel insecure about their job , if their target are not met. Here they have stress about meeting the sales target and losing their job.*

*Balance Sheet: -Balance sheet is the issue of top management of the companies and they are always concerned about the debtors and creditors , which leads to bad debts. In order to meet our sales ,the top management take risks and sell goods on credit ,which leads to increase in debtors. This is the reason of increasing bad debts of companies and banks. The CEOs has many other projects to accomplish and they are always in pressure to complete the projects. All this if not planned and executed properly leads to stress and they fall in to depression and the rest continue.*

*Family :-Every corporate has a family, apart from the corporate responsibility they have family responsibility too, and many of them are not able to fulfill the family expectation. This add more woes in to their pressure. Home is the place where a person comes to take rest after performing his duties at office , and if the atmosphere at home is not supportive we won't be able to relax our mind. This causes sleeping disorder in many corporate. Due to the the stress they are not able to get the required sleep which is required to relax the body and mind. If our stress is not exhausted how come will one be able to perform his duties in the office and meet his corporate goal. All this misbalance leads to depression and if not handled wisely arouses suicidal tendencies in us.*

*Some examples of recent corporate suicide around the world are V. G. Sidhartha of Café coffee day, who in his suicide letter has mentioned that there is enough of fund in the balance sheet to repay the debt; if this was the reason what was the need to end the life. Certainly he needed a right person to make him realize the importance of life.Vineetwhig of Encyclopedia Britanicca's chief ended his life accepting that he was depressed and finds no way but to suicide the list goes on ..*

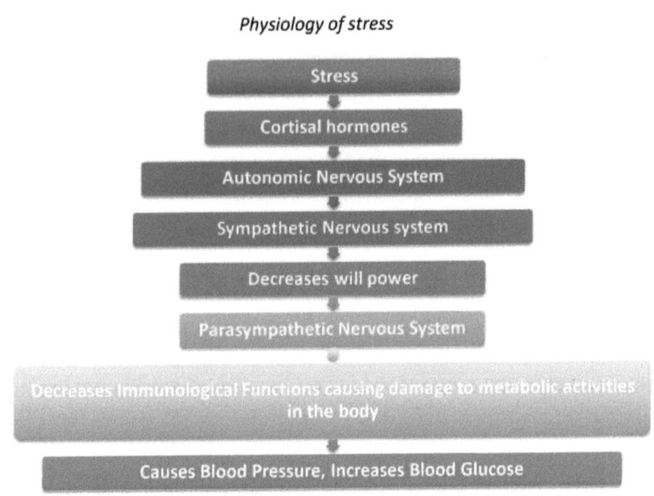


*Depression: Depression in Hindi is called (Awshad). Bhagwatgeeta starts with the chapter Arjunvishad yoga. In the battle field looking at his own men at the forefront Arjun felt depressed and was surrounded by infatuation. Lord Krishna showed him the path by his sermons which gave birth to Bhagwatgeeta. Arjun didn't consulted any psychiatrist in kurukshetra. Lord Krishna words and inspiration was more than enough to bring him out of depression and infatuation.*

*Its mentioned in Valmiki Ramayan when Lakshman became unconscious in the battle field lord ram went in to depression and started thinking about his promises made to vibhishan to coronate him as the king of Lanka and how will he return back home with lakshman dead.*

*Depression is state of mind , being gripped by infatuation because of the modes of nature. And the best way to come out of depression is to come out of infatuation by bringing change in our living habits.*

*We all know that t brain consumes about twenty percent of our body energy which is just as the size of fist. Stress causes the brain to consume more body energy and we feel fatigue very soon. When our energy is low our will power diminishes and we lose with ourselves very quickly.*

*To de stress our mind , come out of depression and uplift our energy level we should adopt the following measures:*

*Meditation: Meditation is the best way to de stress our mind. It has been proved scientifically that Meditation increases the grey matter in the brain which increases the creativity and productivity level in human being.. When we are in stress and depression our brain over thinks which increase the frequency level of the brain. Meditation brings the frequency level of the brain to performing level and increases the performance of brain.*

*Pranayam: it's a breathing technique of inhaling and exhaling. Which enhances the air elements in our body. The slower the breathe the more is our understanding level of our surrounding. When our understanding level is high , we are in a state to take decision quickly.*

*Satsang: Satsang is interaction with the saints, seer or the wise. Interaction with them clears our doubts. We obtain wisdom. when we live without doubt our decision making level gets enhanced. At this level we get to know the real purpose of life, which is not merely the sales target or the corporate projects but life is worth more than that.*

*Sevice: service to the needy sheds our Ego, which indirectly helps in curbing various peer pressure, competitiveness and jealously. all this are enemies of our mind. Therefore one should at regular interval indulge himself in to service to the poor and people in need.*

*Music :- Music plays a big role in detoxifying stress provided its frequency is not above the normal hertz of brain. In Vedas we have different ragas which frequency differs from one other and is made up of according to the different time period of the day.*

*Environment: corporate leaders should create a healthy environment in his office which would de stress the office environment. The employee should have the feeling of belongingness. They should be given flexibility in time. There should be proper arrangements for recreation.*

*Loneliness is a blessing in disguise: loneliness if dealt wisely plays a greater role in enhancing our personality and increasing our knowledge and getting answer to most of our day to day problem. If we spent few minutes regularly and analyze on our problems we get answer to many of our problems and apart from that our mind get time to relax from the worldly chaos. Our sages have praised worthiness of (ekantwaas) loneliness.*

*Advice :- In ancient time when kings or great people used to fail they used to proceed to sages to seek answer to their problems and the sages with their enriched wisdom used to clear the doubts of the concerned person. The saint apart from their wisdom has spiritual energy which affects the person when they communicate with them.*

*If we adopt the above measures we can de stress our mind and enhance our energy level. All this will enhance the will power within us and motivate us to take active responsibilities in our day to day life. It will make us realize the importance of life and bring enthusiasm in life.*

CHAPTER IV

# Entrepreneurship as Experimentation

*Entrepreneurship as defined in vedic scriptures prophets an act which requires endurance with will to obtain any objective. Modern definition of entrepreneurship describes it as act through which one ventures in to any business activities as per a plan and prescribed measures to obtain profit. Obviously every venture is started with a motive to earn profit, if not everyone should be doing some charity and I wonder from where will the funds come , if profit is not accrued from business.*

*Experimentation: Entrepreneurial experimentation requires a thought process and action there on to obtain the desire objective. It might happen that we does not succeed in the entrepreneurial venture but remember that those efforts and journey will certainly give you some lesson which you might need in future course of your life. Every experiments involves some process and so does the entrepreneurial experimentation, it doesn't matter how big the investment is but certainly apart from the profit , even you don't succeed you gain some experience, who knows might be helpful in some other venture at some other point of time.*

*The theory of entrepreneurship revolves around the scarcity in the society of which the nation and the whole world constitute of. Since we start from the scarce there lies a lot of uncertainty and risk in venturing in to the new project. It's a common feeling about the consumption of the product in the market. It requires a lot of study about consumer preference and demand of the project in the market.*

*Entrepreneurial venture requires a deep study on product and customer discovery. Since these are the two areas on which any ventures depend. And as a entrepreneurial experimentation we have to focus on this two areas which decides the viability of any ventures.*

*Every experiment constitutes of hypothesis and on success of it results a theory. So at first we have to work on the hypothesis we have derived and testify it whether it succeeds or not.*

*A man who aspires to wealth or craves to rise high must give up the following six undesirable traits –*

*1.Excessive sleep 2. Lassitude 3.Fear 4.Anger 5.Laziness 6.Procrastination -Vidur*

*In Sanskrit there is a couplet which says to obtain wealth one should have the enduring qualities of a lion. Wealth comes to one who is always engaged in hard work. A lion never depends up on other for food and it's always engaged in efforts.*

*Skills required*

*Endurance:- Lord Krishna states in Shreemadbhagwatam that the greatest victory is winning over our true nature. We should remember that endurance is the true nature of a human. We should always be engaged in performing action and there should be continuity in the action performed. In the corporate world we might face many obstacles and difficulties, dirty tricks by rivals to pull you down , there would come a time when we would have to meet failures but inspite of all this you should have that will power to stand and start performing again. Failures should be taken as a lesson learnt and we should move on with a fresh zeal and endeavor.*

*Design Thinking:- Design thinking comes from Natural abilities, natural and creative intelligence. Here I have mentioned natural abilities because every human being have different set of skiil which defines his or her abilities . we just need to discover that skills with which we are at best and turn that skill in to ability and than that ability in to a profit making venture.We need to have perpetual acuity- ie.. to see things around corner and spot potentiality in others and nature. Analyzing and interpreting on the thought process results in to design thinking.*

*Creative Problem solving:- The origin of any entrepreneurial venture begins with a problem to solve and if we are not equipped with it we won't succeed on the path of entrepreneurship .An entrepreneur should be a problem solver. He should be able to solve the problem with his perpetual acuity skills.*

*Opportunity for an entrepreneur always lies in the scarcity and problems present in the society and he has to pick the right one as per his skills and recourses available to him. Just imagine if you are given a biscuit of gold and asked to make a product out of it, everyone would think that whatever we make out of it, it would cost just as the cost of gold present in the market, but an optimist might think of making a design out of it which is not present in the market and that would fetch him more than the cost of gold. The extra price he fetched is of the design and it was his thought and forward thinking ability.*

*Risk taking ability:- An entrepreneur should posses the risk taking ability. He should always have the willingness to take calculated risk. He should have the deep knowledge and skills required for the concerned venture which would give him the farsightedness to foresee the future challenges and opportunity in the said venture.*

*Forward Thinking:-An entrepreneur should have forward thinking skills. He should be an optimist and after looking and weighing on both the aspect of any problem should always look at the brighter side of it. In analyzing a problem many a time we keep on focusing on the past happenings which might not happen again and if we try to solve any problem without looking forward it might always stand before as a problem and a challenges and could never be solved. Therefore an entrepreneur should always look forward and find a solution to the problem.*

*Business model development: can we experiment any idea without having any method, perhaps we need to have a method through which we are going to solve the problem. This is called business model development. This is the beginning of any venture. At this level we develop the plan through which we are going to solve the problems. The model contains amount of capital required , sources of fund, land, labor, human resources, customer, product market etc...the entrepreneur need to prepare the feasibility plan of the business.*

*Harnessing Recourses :- For any business venture the three main necessities are land labour and capital. When it comes to harnessing it primarily emphasize on human resource and capital. An entrepreneur if doesn't have the financial and human resource knowledge should hire an expert in the above field who could harness the resources for the enterprise. Any enterprise runs on capital and revolves around the human resource and these two things are needed to be harness efficiently and wisely.*

*Marketing and customer acquisition: - Any entrepreneurial venture exists because of its product, because it's the product for which the venture has been established. The question here arise of selling and distribution of products which the enterprise produce. There should be proper channel of logistics for supply chain. There should proper study of market regarding consumer preference and income level. Consumer demand is derived from their preference and income and utility of the product at a given period of time. Time plays a significant role in influencing demand because consumer taste and preference keeps on changing as per climate and other factor and because of cardinal utility theory of economy. So there has to be regular research on taste and preference of consumer in the market.*

*Raising money:- funding is a challenging task but not that much if our ides are viable and profitable. The only criteria to be fulfilled is that the investor should be convinced of the feasibility and viability of the venture. Following are some of the means to fund any venture.*

*Venture Capital:- venture capital is the invest in which a capitalist when satisfied with your business model agrees to invest in to your venture at an agreed share of equity in your venture. In venture capital the ownership remains with the entrepreneur and the capital are injected by the venture capitalist for an agreed share in the venture. In India venture capital is regulated by SEBI and detail can be obtained from its website.*

*Start up loan:-many banks provide business loan. Indian Govt. provides start up loan and Mudra loan for new idea and young entrepreneur.*

*Business Incubator:-A business incubator is an organization which provides, consulting, knowledge, and fund for your project in lieu of equity in your venture.*

*Angel Investors:- Angel investor are individual or investor who fund your venture in lieu of equity in your venture. Angel investor uses their own money for investment on the other hand venture capitalist invests through capital from invest companies.*

*Partnership:-partnership is also a means through which the desired number of people can fund any venture with blend of equity and loan.*

*There are six situation in which one is happy*

*1.Freedom from sickness 2.freedom from debt 3.not living away from ones home 4. Company of noble person 5. Living on ones own earning 6. leading a fearless life.*

*In Sanskrit there is a word called* **swalamban***which means self dependent. And this and should be the best way to earn money and fulfill our worldy desires with regards to wealth. Having our own venture has no limit of earning money , it all depends up on our efficiency and management capabilities to what extent our enterprise can flourish.*

*Who knows your experiment might turn out to be a life changing experience for you.*

CHAPTER V

# Stress, Cross Group relation and its affect on performance

*To achieve any goal or accomplish various projects an organization needs human resource with varied expertise which most of the time belongs to various culture and ethnicity. Multinational companies hire human resource from different countries and their projects, when out of home countries requires personnel from that very country where the project is being executed. In such circumstances cross group relation hold prominent importance.*

*In India many companies has employees from various states who speaks different languages and has varied culture.*

*A group is formed by individuals working together to achieve a common goal. Cross functional team consists of different functional expertise working together for a common goal. It includes employees from various levels of organization.*

*Relation in human being consists of union between different people. The cross group relation comprises of union between different groups in an organization or among various organization.*

*Relationship depends up on various human traits which varies among groups depending up on various factors. Some of the factors could be as follows:-*

*Attitude: Attitude is our intent or mental inclination which constitute the different qualities in us. It has major impact of the environment in which we live. Our nature is largely dependent up on our attitude and in cross group relationship we have to deal with people from different culture coming from different background some times stranger to one another and in such scenario it becomes utmost importance.*

*Trust: It's that human trait on which the foundation of any relationship revolves. Without trust a relationship always hovers in doubt. And when we have doubt on the people with whom we are working we will have various barriers in our performance on which the project accomplishment depends. The biggest barrier in lack of trust is communication. human being tends to be open and sharing only when we have confident in the people with whom we are working. If we have even an iota of doubt about the trustworthiness of the personnel with whom we are working, human being hides the secrets. A communication barrier only hampers the performance of the group. Therefore trust is very much importance for performance appraisal of the team. Behaviour:- How we behave with our counterparts in the group decides our behavior.Our behavior depends up the qualities we possess. It depends up on various factors such as our verbal communication, attitude,vibes,thought process , expression , emotion etc.*

*Expectation: - human being has a tendency that we expect from others. Whenever there is dissimilarities among the group our expectation doesn't meets and its effects the behavior across the group.*

*One thing which we should remember is that our expression and vibes matter most in our behavior than verbal words. Because expression dictates authenticity.*

*There are many theories such as social identity theory and self categorization theory which prophet about cross group relation. But to me since building relationship is an art and it varies from person to place we cant and should not depend up on theory rather we should depend up on our subconscious mind for building an everlasting relationship and trust among the group.*

*Some study shows that Americans trust more ingroup members where as Japanese trust more out-group members than Americans. The study reveals one thing that is Japanese are more adaptive than Americans. Our perception also matters a lot in the cross group relation ,since our reciprocal expression depends much up our perception i.e.. how we perceive the things. Therefore to be successful in cross group relation we need to be more adaptive.*

*There is a theory which describes about number of subordinates we can have directly reporting to one personnel. I don't believe in such theory, true that we have a limited working hour in a day and subsequently in months and year and accordingly we have to deal with various people and perform other duties. Thus time may restrict us with how many people or subordinate we can directly report to us certainly not other things. Its time management and communicative skills and knowledge which decides how much subordinate one can has reporting under him. Rest things have to be undermined.*

*To sum up its group dynamic which deals with the attitude and behavior patterns of group Stress:- stress in biological terms means body's method of reacting to condition such as threat challenge or physical or psychological barrier.*

*While working in a team there are a lots of challenges before a group like project completion time limit, sales target, budget constraint and various other environmental and political barriers .all this puts pressure on performance. When er are in stress there is some physiological changes in the brain as a results thereof the productivity level of the brain decreases .a decrease in productivity level diminishes the output of the group.*

*Performance depends up on the following factors*

*Skill: skill is the smallest unit of performance by which we accomplish any job. It's the skill which is required to accomplish any work and rest comes there after.I have seen many mechanics at the service centers of various motor companies who doesn't hold any qualification but has mastered the knowledge of motor parts and its functions through their skills. It's through skills by which we obtain knowledge.*

Attitude:- Attitude is our intent or Natural inclination towards which our minds is always inclined . Our skills are largely influenced by our attitude.

*Knowledge:- knowledge is the second best ingredients or we can say the components in the performance . we can obtain knowledge from various texts and information available on Google, but In order to utilize that we need skills.*

*Its better we obtain knowledge in the field in which possess the best skills. knowledge makes a master, skills makes an expert.*

*Zeal:- Zeal is an stimulus which inspires us from within. It's something to be self developed. In order to have the zeal in the work the first criteria is that your natural instinct and intelligence should allow you to work in that particular field. Obviously it should match your skill and knowledge.*

*Motivation:- motivation is an external stimulus which has influence by or through some external substances may be our team leader or our colleagues. Both zeal and motivation enhances the performance.*

*Environment: it's the surrounding in which we work, it consists of members in the group and constitute of their behavior, Nature and place.*

*Effects of stress on performance and cross group relation.*

*1.Stress secretes cortisol hormones in the brain which changes various human behavior such as tolerance capabilities, memory, analyzing creativity etc..*

2. *stress bring fatigue and lower self esteem bringing the performance level down*
3. *Change in behavior brings mistrust among cross Group relation*
4. *Mistrust creates a sense of doubt*
5. *Doubt diminishes the faith among cross group relation*

*Therefore stress indirectly plays a major role on the performance of cross group relation.*

CHAPTER VI

# Management of work and non work life

*Does prosperity dwells only with professional success? To the riches?*

*I tell you I have met many people personally who have rose to sheer height in their career, but has been struggling to get married, if you think success and money brings prosperity in life and family, forget it! In my astrological consultation I deal with many work and non work problems and people ask me about various family problems which is indirectly connected with their spouse availability of time with their family!*

*There has been growing corporate suicide and CEOs suffering from depression all this are mismanagement of work and non work life.*

*We get married and subsequently become father.*

*Ask one honest question to yourself if you don't have time for your family than why did you got married at all?*

*If satisfying sexual pleasure is only the motive than that can be done by other means , though morally wrong but legally right in many countries.*

*Than why at all we get married? In western world you fall in love and subsequently get married only to discover few years later that those love merely attraction! And then proceeding towards the court for divorce!*

*In Hindu scriptures we marry because four reason*

1. *Women are consider embodiment of peace and men in ancient time had to do outdoor activities , being tired work women were there companion who helped them come out*

*of fatigue. In modern days were women equally contributes in most of the family either in the family business or doing some job .it becomes important for them not to loose the feminine quality. I not only support but encourage and motivate women workforce but not at the cost of feminine quality.*

2. *The other reason for marriage are getting children's and performing action*
3. *Earning Wealth*
4. *Salvation*

*Wondering why I mentioned all this! , just to make you realize the importance of your family and children which according to you constitute your non work life; sorry for me its another responsibility*

*Now that you all have understood the importance of family and children lets come to the main topic how to manage work and non work life. Here the measures by which we can manage work and non work life*

*Management of work and non work life starts with*

*Prioritizing:- Its performing action as per urgency and importance. There might come a situation in life specially for the entrepreneurs and business leaders that at the stroke of the mid night one has to leave the house and attend the work, subsequently a time might come where one has to live the office and attend to family, simultaneously there might arrive a situation where we might be having work at both the end in that case we might prioritize and perform both the action depending up on the urgency. So in prioritizing we have to give importance to the value of work weigh it pros and cons and than prioritize which one is importance.*

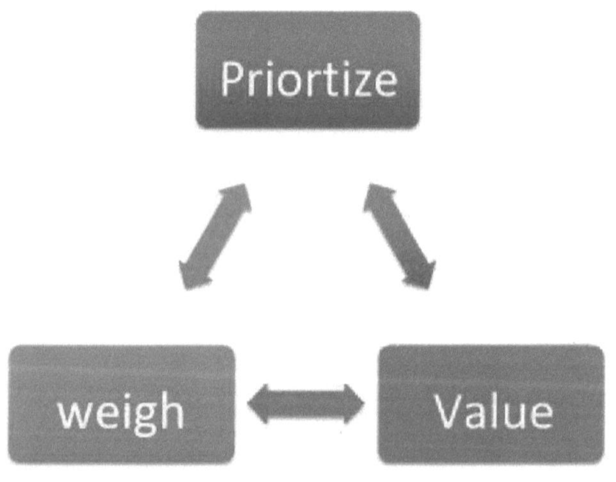


*After priortizzing comes the importance of planning . you might ask me why am I mentioning planning , the answer is we have 24 hours in a day and in that you need at least 5 hours of sleep, we spent at least 2 hours for daily routine such as*

*breakfast, lunch dinner and for fresh and change. Now we have just 17 hours left for work in a day. Out of seventeen hours most of you spent 8 hours in hours in office and a minimum of 1 hour in travelling. Now you have only 8 hours left*

*Remember those people have the plan for this 8 hours rise to the top level and achieve great success.*

*Do spent at least a hour with your children and family no matter how busy your life. Its not only your duty but also your responsibility. your children are also the future of nation and if you give time to them and groom them , they will obviously raise your name in the society simultaneously they will be equally contribute to the nation and the world. So do keep time for your family and children. No matter how busy you are.*

*In short I am mentioning the elements involved in planning*

*Start with your goal which you want to achieve, gather information about your goal, analyze on the gathered information, prioritize it and decide what steps are required to obtain the goal, find the measure or the means through which you can achieve the set steps now that you have a plan , information , steps and measure or means to achieve the goal, move on to the steps through the measures adopted and continuously monitor the steps because it's the steps that will lead you to the goal.*

*Resources to a large extent play a major role in prioritizing. If we don't have the resources what and how can we prioritize, the question here arises how we can have the resources. The simplest way is to go for financial planning and inculcate a habit of saving regularly from your earning. You all should have at least the basic knowledge of financial planning. More ever the planning process remains the same, saving depends up o your income and you should have a certain percentage of your income as a contingent asset.*

*Flexibility :- there might come a circumstance or situation where you might not have been able to accomplish your objective as per your plan in that case you should have the flexibility to postpone some of your plan to some other time or day and subsequently in the planned time you could some other future planned work. This future course of action proponed will let you do the work which you have postponed at that very time. Like this you won't waste your time and neither your plan will fail. Thus there should be flexibility the planned work and various other measures in life. Remember flexibility doesn't mean that you do unethical and immoral activities. That might land you in trouble, so beware of those shortcuts before executing it.*

*To conclude management of work and non work life depends up on prioritizing and planning. We need to have a sound life style and understand the value of family at home and family at office. Certainly both are family we have to maintain the balance between both by sensing the importance of what is to be done when by weighing the value of the work through duty and responsibility required to be performed as per the need of time of situation and circumstances.*

CHAPTER VII

# Product discovery process

*Product is that matter of a enterprise on which their business exists .Every functions and activities of a business organization whether it's in service or manufacturing sector depends up on the product they produce.*

*One might argue that we need finance to run the business activities, to an extent you are right but beyond that it's the product that will fetch you the money and not the money will fetch you the product.*

*If you think business runs only on finance and if you have enough of currency than better apply for a bank license to the central bank of your country; but could you answer me how will you multiply you money which you are investing in your bank, obviously banks sole source of income is interest and to whom will you grant a loan? Do you think a charitable organization will apply for a loan and pay you interest? Perhaps never, certainly you will invest in a business enterprise that's in sound state and earning profit and to new startups who has profitable ideas! So profit is the sole motive of business and that's earned from the product you produce.*

*Hope you could differentiate between the importance of product and money.*

*Now that we have understood the importance of product lets understand what product is and on what does the origin of products depends.*

*A product is a goods or services which has some utility, the utility has some value and that value san be exchanged for money which is called sales.*

*Before getting in to the process of product discovery lets distinguish between the existing product and new product. Existing companies has their set of product and their business run on that. A new enterprise has some ideas about a product which many a time are different from existing product and if at all they plan to sell the existing product than certainly there is scarcity of that very product in the market which the new entrepreneur thinks would fetch them profit.*

*Why do we need product discovery?*

*Cardinal utility theory of economics states that with every decrease in the price of commodities their demand increases but after a certain level when there are satisfied with that very product, their consumption decreases. Demand also depends up on taste and preference of consumer, climate, festivity and many other factors.*

*From cardinal utility its very clear that after certain period of time our intent to consume a particular product gets satisfied since we has have derived the maximum utility from it, hence consumer starts looking for a change , economist says human being are rationale . Hence our taste and preferences keeps on changing.*

*These are the reason many good business enterprise has R&D department which looks specifically on product innovation and discovery.*

*In product discovery Consumer is the Focal point.*

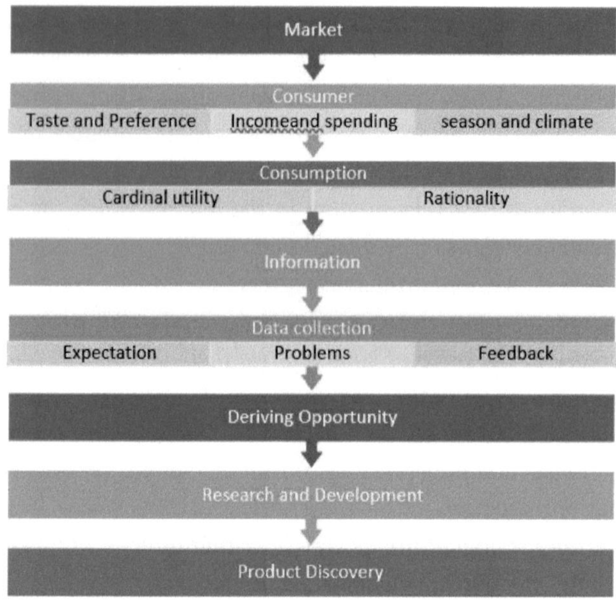


*Product Discovery Process.*

*Market: It's a place where the value of product is derived by selling it for money to the consumer. Consumer is the unit of market. Journey of products ends here with deriving the objective of production.it's the micro segments of economy. Every monetary policy exists as per the status of well being market.*

*Consumer: a consumer is a living being who consumes any product or service for its utility in lieu for money.*

*Taste and preferences:- Taste and preference keeps on changing and the current taste and preferences should be studied through a strong feed back system. If any enterprise has the knowledge of current taste and preferences of consumer and they know that it has change they could quickly discover a new product keeping in view of the customer recent preference.*

*Income and spending:- consumption of a product depends up on spending of consumer and spending depends up on income . An enterprise always has to keep an eye on the current income and spending of the consumer. A higher spending not only increases the demand rather consumer demands shift to higher level segment because of status symbol. A shift in income will increase the demand of the best available good status wise in that particular segments.*

*Hence keeping an eye on the expected spending of increased income group with change in taste and preference a company can discover new product for such group, this will not only bring profits to the company but also new customer for their product to whom the company can make them a permanent customer with improved quality and brand value.*

*Climate and season:-It's a basic economic theory that demand depends up on climate and during the festive season demand increases and so on. But due to the rationale behavior consumer expects better product or rather some change in the product even be it the festive season. So a good season with a newer product than the previous season would always fetch a better demand, rather than just waiting for some good festive season.*

*Consumption:- The unit of consumption is the consumer. It's consumer who consume the goods and services. Consumption depends upon the above factors where as opportunity for discovery lies in the below factors of consumption.*

*Cardinal utility:-we all know that after certain level of consuming a particular products specially in the consumer durable goods the utility derived from such product diminishes and hence the demand for it also decreases . In such*

*Rationality:-Human being are rationale being and their consumption are based on the above behavior apart from the necessity goods.*

*Information:- Companies should regularly gather information from the market on the above mentioned areas. The information gathered should be authentic else it would prove to be harmful. now that we have gathered information we should disseminate the data in to following three segments. Information should be gathered on a defined parameters which can be stored as data for further use in research and development.*

*Data : a company should have a data centre where the data of consumer could be stored for further use. If we collect information in a defined parameters it will always shows us the below*

*Problems:- Consumer is the best source to know if at all any problems exist in the product. Various problems received at the service centre of the product, the frequency of the defects in the product and services, would reveal us a common set of defects in the product and services. This defects and problems amount to opportunity on which the company can further look for.*

*Feed back:- Feedback is the best source of information available about the quality and future prospects of the product. A feedback form could be set on such parameters that could reveal us the future expectation of consumer about the product.*

*Expectation:- knowing the future expectancy of the product , the R&D unit can work to find the various scope and field of expectancy to discover new products.*

*Deriving opportunity: Now that we have the data we have to study and analyze the data to find opportunity in it. There should be an in-depth study of data to look for the consumer problems and future expectancy.*

*Research and development: Probably many big companies has R&D department. They should now do research on how to transform the opportunity in to product. Change in consumer taste and preferences leads to new discovery, because consumer has willingness for some other products since the old product has lost its utility value.*

*Some other factors which indirectly affect product discovery process are product substitute, value of brand and advertisement. All this affects the demand indirectly. You can't bring a product in the market which cant compete with the product substitute available in the market. It should either has a better brand value than the close substitute or better quality. Thus brand value and quality are the two things which affects demand indirectly, apart from other aspects of demand; quality to much extent depends up on advertisement. But it's a fact that a brand remains its value so long as it maintains it quality. To maintain the quality there should be continuous research and development adopting the product discovery process.*

*It's here where the process of product discovery ends.*

CHAPTER VIII

# Inequalities in emerging economies

*Think of the Mighty kings who at the end of their glorious reins, leaving behind their kingdoms and the ultimate in luxury they had enjoyed and to surrendered to Yamraj(God of Death). Their treasuries were full. They were Powerful kings. Yet they could not escape death.*

*Vidur advice to king Dhritrashtra ofHastinapur( Now Delhi NCR)*

*The sole reason for the inequalities in World is due to the lack of farsightedness of world leaders and Govt. Policies. They keep worlds best economist from reputed universities as their advisers and the results are in front of everyone.*

*What have we be teaching and learning at universities in and around the world that we have to see such inequalities around the world. United states which has some of the world best universities and intellectuals has such huge inequalities in their country.*

*One economist I personally has a a lots of respect is RaghuramRajan , former*

*Governor of Reserve bank of India and a professor of Finance at Chicago University. He was the one who has predicted way back probably in 2005 about upcoming recession in united states, which indeed occurred in 2008,than many economist were not convinced about it. Apart from his knowledge what I love about him is his frankness and that should be a necessary quality of an advisor.*

*When inequalities grows in a country the first things which emerge is inferiority complex. We are human and due to some of behavioral traits we compare with others. Many of you who didn't get me , Let me prove it, Perhaps we are prepared and bought up in an environment were we begin comparing at home and than at school. We are given marks and grades and we compare marks with our peer students at school and from their to office and so own the process continues perhaps even after death, yes there are many rankings of achievements by many magazines which compares billionaire, scientists, thinkers ,sportsperson, so they are not going to stop that comparison even after death.*

*This comparison when widens brings some sorts of injustice and feeling of inferiority and creates sense of insecurity and doubt among the citizen.*

*A doubting soul Perishes –Lord Krishna*

*A true leader should erase the sense of doubt prevailing their citizens, and this can be done by appropriate govt. policies.*

*Let us look at some of the Factors which has bought inequalities in economies around the world.*

1. *Lack of Skills*
2. *Economic Ignorance*
3. *Lack of Resources*
4. *Policy Implementation*

*To me apart from govt. policies these four factors had played major role in growing inequalities around the world.*

***Skills** are more important than knowledge; perhaps one can achieve mastery only in the area in which he possesses the skills. Its skill that propels us to acquire knowledge in that very field.Skills has direct relation with our nature.*

*In India lack of government policy by previous Govt. about the youth has had an large impact on their livelihood. It's a great step by the present govt. which has understood the importance of skill and formed skill India ministry. If implemented properly this scheme will prove to be a boon for India's youth and unemployed citizens.*

2.**Economic Ignorance**:-*Ignorance is the root of failure. Ignorance arises out of inaction and idleness. Due to lack of proper Govt. policy their citizens lived in idleness and inaction resulting to ignorance. Those with lower income group didn't active part in countries economic activities resulting in to economic ignorance.*

3.**Lack Of Resources**:-*economically backward citizens lacks resources such as wealth and human resources which became restraint in their progress. For success you need a plan with resources to fulfill that plan if either one lack your plan wont work and you fail.*

4. **Policy Implementation**:-*Due to lack of talent in bureaucracy and corruption there has been failure in the implementation of policies resulting into wastage of nation wealth in corruptions and valuable time of citizen and wastage of a huge number of human potential which could have been turned in to nation asset had policy been implemented properly. Unfortunately at present all has become a liability.*

*Repercussion of growing inequalities in some of countries around the world.*

*Recently there has been yellow vest moment in France demanding for economic justice. There has been countrywide protest by these activities burning restaurants and shops.*

*In world happiness report 2019 and world competitive report 2019. People has people were more concerned with freedom to choose. People from Hongkong , Santiago were has been recent protests all has one common motive economic injustice and freedom to choose.*

**Warning:- The** *leaders around the world has to take appropriate measure to Narrow the inequalities else it might* *have a major impact on well being of their nation if not consequentially it will increase sense of insecurity in the nation.*

*A advice to those leaders from the words of Chanakya*

*Righteousness is the root of Prosperity.*

*Now let us find the measure through which we can curb and Narrow Inequalities.*

*Government policy.In Vedic scriptures citizens are considered as children of the king. We live in democratic world and we have a elected government, if not son at least the modern leaders should consider their citizens as their family members. This will prevail the sense of belongingness among the citizens and the leader. It's not only the responsibility of government but a fundamental duty to prevail social and economic justice to their citizens. Govt. should adopt following measures to bring equality in society*

***Separate Budget for skill Development** :-Govt. should have separate allocation of fund in their budget to promote skills of their citizens. Skills should be promoted on the basis of ones inherent and natural intelligence. There should be aptitude test for knowing their intent and mental inclination. To know about mental inclination set a questionnaire about their preference, perception, behavioral traits , likes and dislikes about places , person and few other objects which could reveal their true nature.*

**Promoting merit: - Every***recruitment and promotion in the country should me on merit based and person with merit should be given due respect, irrespective of their financial well being, caste, creed or religion.*

**Equal Opportunity:-***Govt. should frame a policy which provides equal opportunity for every citizens irrespective of caste , creed, religion, race, color.*

***Promoting Entrepreneurship:-*** *Govt. should provide Tax holidays or rebate in tax for economically backward entrepreneurs. Financial support for start upsventures.this will encourage entrepreneurial environment in the economy. The Govt. specially in the developing countries which has large number of youth unemployed they should implement such policies, any way they don't come under your tax net so they won't affect your revenue base , but if they at all gain vigor for self dependency which is possible on encouragement than certainly if not today but some day in future they will certainly become a honest tax payer. At present by the policy they will not pay the Govt. corporate tax but certainly they will earn income on which they will pay tax if they come under the taxable base. Even they don't come under the taxable net, they will become self dependent and for a govt. this should be their first priority that their citizen becomes self dependent. One small venture will certainly employee more than one people like wise this would create series of employment and more people getting employed and self dependent.*

*Transform education system:- Blend of practical and theoretical education right from primary school to higher education. Scholarship and loan at affordable rate and flexible repayment terms. Intellectual level of Nation increases.*

*Higher education:- There should be proper counseling and guidance provided to youth about the importance of higher education. They should be made aware of the various options available to them after higher education in various field.*

*Financial literacy:- There are many people who though are literate are unaware of the financials analogy. They should be made financially aware so that they can invest and multiply their wealth. They should be made aware of the option available in the financial markets such as stocks and mutual fund.*

*Freedom To Choose: Level of our knowledge is never judged from the degree you posses rather from the experience you have gained by working on your skills. Therefore the more skills you have the more option you have. People should have various opportunities in the country to pursue their skill and fulfill what they choose or desire.*

*Competitive Environment: Country which has competition law should ensure that its implemented properly on the ground and no one should be given undue influence by the Govt. every one has the right to earn money but not at the cost of others opportunity and rights. Govts. Should ensure that the dominance of rich corporate doesn't hamper the competition in the country and every one has equal opportunity to pursue their dream. They must ensure that the small entrepreneurs doesn't get bullied away by the existing corporate who money wise can influence and obstain the new comers in the market.*

*Role of Rich:- The Rich could play a major role in creating the entrepreneurial environment in the country provide they are shouldered the responsibility. They could be encourage to fund startups in the country, setting up institution of entrepreneurship, traininq etc.*

*Earning money is not a crime so long as it is legally and*

*ethically earned. If someone has become rich through legal and ethical way he should be respected and encouraged. They should not be harassed , if so would be immoral , unethical and illegal. The Govt. should have good relation with the corporates , they should have the feeling that their leader is listening to them and care about them. This will create a sense of trust among corporate and the Govt. all their worthy demands should be fulfilled . Only think that has to be cautious about is Impartiality . The leader should be impartial , if the corporate need any sorts of advice, help it should be met but with a sense of impartiality.*

*By adopting such measures the Govt. Can bring down the inequality in the nation and worldwide.*

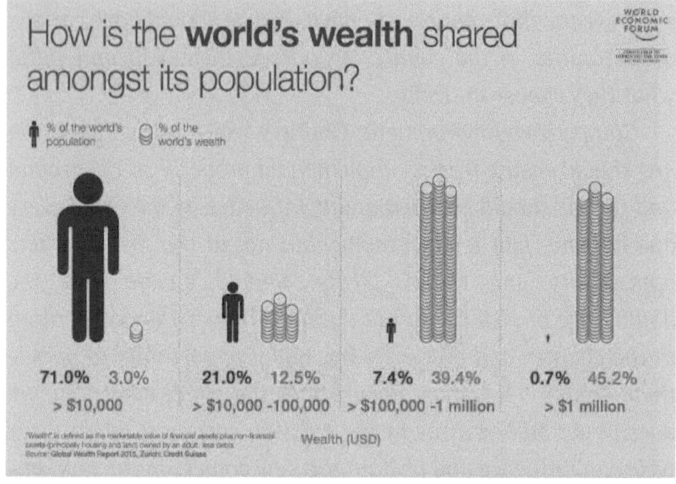

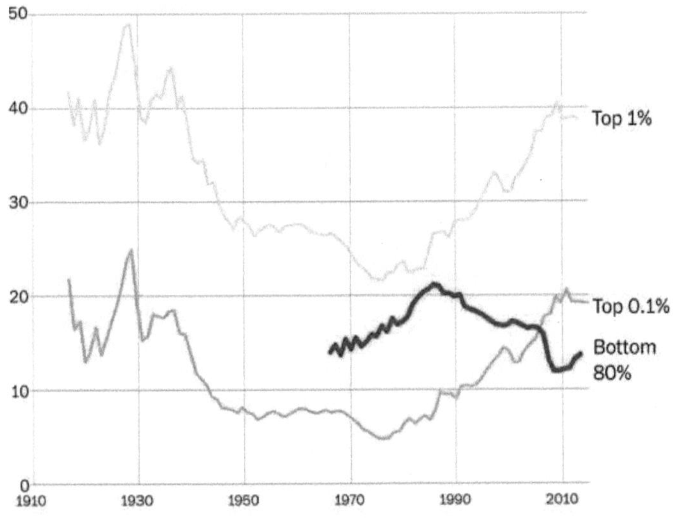
The top 0.1% now own more than the bottom 80%
Share of American wealth owned by the top 1%, the top 0.1%, and the bottom 80% of American adults
50
40
30
20
10
0
1910
1930
1950
1970
1990
2010
Top 1%
Top 0.1%
Bottom 80%
Sources: Gabriel Zucman, World Inequality Database
THE WASHINGTON POST

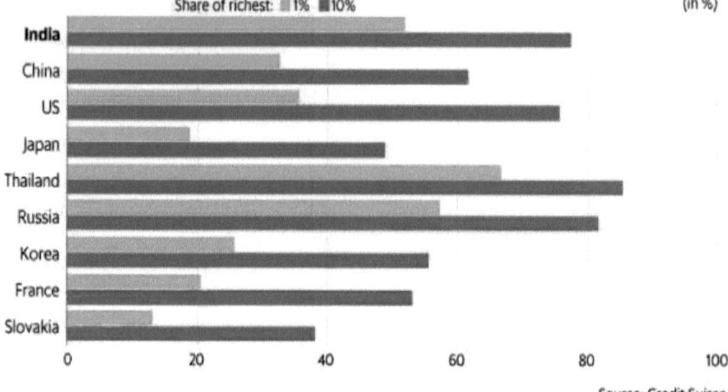
Chart 2
India among high-inequality nations
Slovakia has the least wealth inequality.
Share of richest: 1% 10%
(in %)
India
China
US
Japan
Thailand
Russia
Korea
France
Slovakia
0
20
40
60
80
100
Source: Credit Suisse

CHAPTER IX

# Housing scheme policy; A Necessity

*House : For me It's a place where one can throw away the worldly nuisance and relax and recreate themselves with family which provide safety and security for life .Then comes the place which protects us from Various natural activities such as heat, rain, wind .Apart from above it's a place and should be place were one could attain peace.*

*A proper house according to me should be a necessity. Homelessness provides a sense of insecurity. When a person lives in insecurity, they always live in a dilemma about their future course of life. A doubting soul cannot obtain success in life and such people life becomes useless. Those people with homelessness specially the youths, becomes a liability for the nation.*

*Recently there has been increase in homelessness around the world.*

*Every Night around 60000 people sleep in the municipal shelter system up 43% from 10 years ago.*

*The number of people sleeping rough on the street of paris is on rise. According to France national institute of statics and economic studies more than 12000 people sleep on the streets of France.*

*As per 2011 census of India 57000 people remained homeless. Women Accounts for 25 percent of the Mumbai homeless population.*

*There has been 13.7% percent increase in homelessness in Australia.*

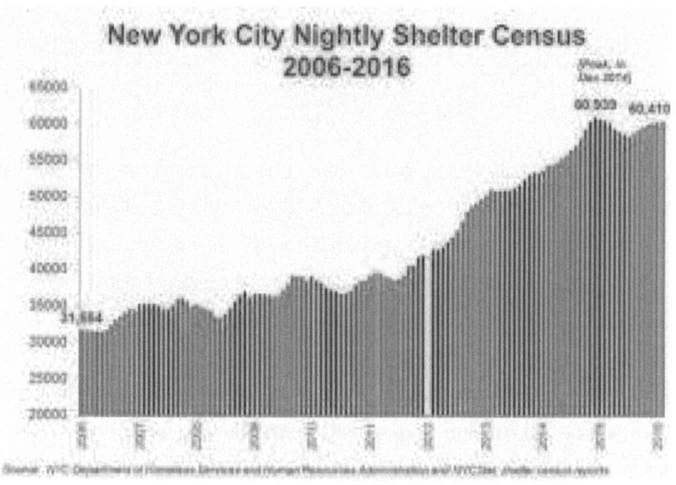


There has been a 28% increase in Australians aged 55+ experiencing homelessness. They are a rapidly growing age bracket

- ABS Census, 2016

**Homelessness in Australia has increased 13.7% in 5 years**

- ABS Census, 2016

*Evils Of homelessness*

*Homelessness creates the following evils*

*Social Injustice: - A sense of Injustice prevails in the area where majority of the population are homeless.*

*Economic Inequalities:- At a time when majority of population are economically living a life of satisfaction, it is injustice being done to them by the government. It's the responsibility of the Government to provide the basic necessities to the marginal section of society who are economically insufficient and dependent on others. They have a feeling of economic inequality.*

*Wastage of human Potential:- People who are homeless are mostly dependent up on other for their livelihood. They mostly work in the unskilled labour sector. They are mostly hand to mouth, as such their childrens has no future prospects if they remain like this. As such its wastage of prospects of their children potential, if they fail to provide them proper education. As such it will be wastage of human potential.*

*Social Miscreants:- A person unemployed and homeless can be bribed , lured do illegal activities for easy money which would create disturbance and affects peace in the society. As such they would live as s social miscreants and nothing more than that. This will impact the well being of normal citizens.*

*Corruption:- In one or the other way such people unknowingly out of their compulsion breeds corruption, either in election or by some other means. It's just because they can be bribed if not can be threatened out of their compulsion*

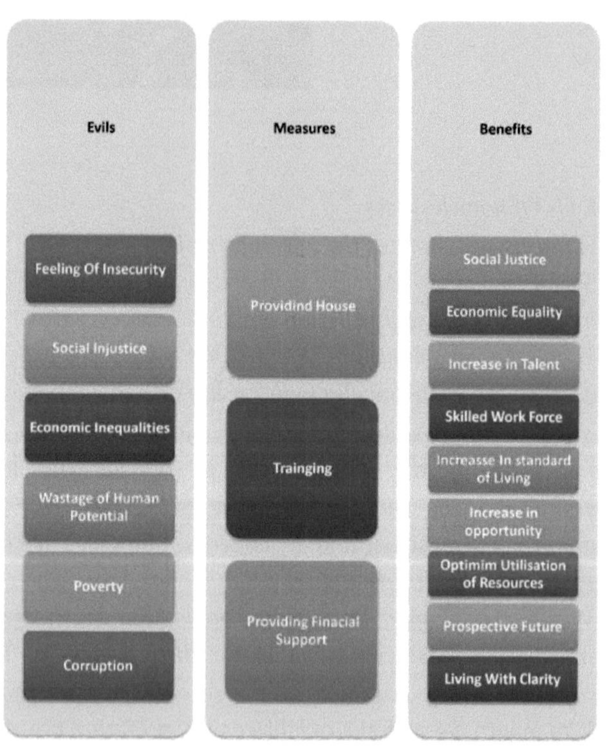

*Economies Of Affordable housing schemes*

*Why should Government in countries with homelessness spend on housing scheme such as providing subsidy on price of house, free home and subsidy on interest on loan for building home in the urban area?*

*Affordable Housing scheme has Social Cost Benefits. For a Government, Social cost matters since it indirectly affects the economy in many ways. In India Government of India provides Rs.1.25 Lakhs to a house hold for building a Home. Assume That Govt. Of India spends Rs.1 Billion on affordable housing scheme with that spending around 8000 house can be built. If we assume one house hold has 4 members than the scheme has provided hours to 32000 citizens. Assume that .If we further assume that out of this 32000 there are 50% of person who can be employed if they are provided skills and training, they will enter the job market and entrepreneurial forum enriching and increasing the talent market. This will increase the competitiveness in the economy. Their happiness level of the society will increase. They will have more option to choose. Their children's will have a far better life than their predecessor.*

*Impact of affordable housing scheme on economy.*

*Since housing scheme raises the standard of living of beneficiaries and if we provide proper training and skill the employable they will enter in to economic activities. If those people were working in the labor force or as non skilledlabor , after obtaining skills they will earn more than before , if some educated employable person enters in to entrepreneurial venture , he or she will enjoy few people like wise employability in the market will increase. The per capita of the country will increase.*

*Today might be this employable youth or the prospective doesn't pay taxes, since many might not come under the taxable base, but some day if provided proper entrepreneurial environment they prosper they might become active taxpayer. The citizens which were your liability now has turned in to countries asset.*

*The aspiration of this people rises, their expectation rises and if provided proper employability sources their spending increases.*

*Life standard of senior citizen*

*The life standard of the senior citizen improves and they feel themselves secure about their old age. They are more satisfied about their future generation.*

*Human beings are influenced by various emotions which influence their feelings. A homeless person always has various sorts of insecurity like weather, climate, anti social miscreants. They have concern regarding their belongings, life threats etc. Having our own house gives us a feeling of security and when our life is secure in terms of house at least we can rest and sleep with ease and carry on our day to day affairs from the house. At least from here on they can think and plan about their future generation.*

CHAPTER X

# Poverty eradication in women in global economy

*To born poor is an Incident but to die Poor is an accident. To born poor might be a compulsion but to die poor is a sin.*

***Poverty***

*Being an astrologer I am an ardent supporter of Democracy, because in astrology the whole solar system is governed on the Principal of*

*Decentralization and delegation of authority assigned to various planets, and The king and Minister Changes every Year.*

*Many of you believe in destiny, Perhaps me to an extent, but you know the whole principle of astrology revolves around action and Only action and nothing less than that and nothing more than that.*

*Why am I saying about this is because those of you who believe in Rebirth,*

*Destiny in your next birth will be based on the action you perform in this birth!*

*So why blame? Just accept things as it and continue on the path of action, certainly some day you might be able to change your destiny. Yes! In history people have changed their destiny but that's not that easy*

***Women***

*There has been talk about women mentioned in Manusmriti and many people oftenly quote about it and defame our scriptures. But that's only the negative aspects of women you are speaking of and also about our scriptures.*

*There are many positive aspects of women mentioned in the Vedic scriptures and few of those are:*

*Women is the most Pious creature of God*

- *Mahabharat*

*Women resides in the whole universe. They are the cause of your existence*

- *Durgasaptsati*

*Seducing a trusting women is considered as killing a Brahmin (Intellectual, a saint) -Vidur*

*He who condemns a women un necessarily meets to hell – Vidur*

*In Vedas wome is considered as Janani( Progenerator) they are the cause of our existence.*

*Hence every effort should be made to bring them in to mainstream of life, since they are the progenitor ,the quality of their progeny will depend up on their quality of their well being at the time of progenesis. Their progeny will be the future citizens of the nation.*

*World bank and UN report on Poverty in women.*

*As of 2013 estimated 767 million people lived below the international poverty line of $1.90 a day. Result shows that between the age of 20 and 34 years women are more likely to be more poor than men. Divorced women in the age of 18-49 are group more than twice as likely to be poor than men. Research shows that household with children are among the poorest and the single parents with children and predominantly single mother with children face a far higher risk of poverty. The study revealed that the place where these women perform their work had affected not only their health* *but also the well being of their children.*

*Cause of Poverty in Global Economy*

*Gender Discrimination:-This is the most common cause of poverty around the world. Due to discrimination they are not allowed to go out of their home and work to earn their livelihood. I*

*Racial Discrimination. In this world women are generally discriminated on the basis of their color of their skin, religion, caste creed and religion. Due to this many women either don't work or if they do they have to do menial job for uncompetitive wages with a sense of inferiority. They always live in a low self esteem.*

*Unorganized Labour market: such women are paid low wages due to their compulsion, many of them are unpaid for their work and many of them have to work overtime to fulfill their daily target of money.*

*Homelessness:- Majority of women specially living in slums does not have their home. They always live in a temporary set ups like huts and tents or on the streets under sky.*

*Mobility for livelihood:- Due to lack of source of income in their areas they mostly keep on shifting from one place to another for a better wages .This generate mobility in them and they are not able to stay at one place because cyclic and seasonal labor type work force, they mostly work in agriculture farms*

.

*Illiteracy:- Women who live in poverty are almost illiterate, and they pay the price for their for their illiteracy by doing menial job.You can't teach them how to read or write, perhaps it's very difficult because they have crossed the age were they would be able to learn and write. Exceptions are always there.*

*Lack of Awareness:-Most of them are not aware of the happenings in the society. They are not aware of the Govt.*

*policy. They live in ignorance. They don't know the value of human potential. They don't have the feeling of importance of and prospects of their children. Their children are malnourished and most of the time stunted. Lack of awareness diminishes the prospects of their future generation, though they are poor and they have little option yet that should not be the excuse when it comes to parenting.*

*Dependency:- Due to Gender discrimination they mostly depend up on the male counterpart and are probably not allowed to join the labor work force. Probably this would amount to opportunity loss if at all they are willing to and have work to perform. Had they been working at least it could have to an extent lessen the burden of their family and would have had a bit of few option to exercise.*

*Research shows that household with children are among the poorest and that single parents with children and predominantly single mother and children face a far higher risk of poverty*

*Policy for Eradication of poverty in women*

*Literacy Programme: Frankly speaking, after you cross 32 if till than happened learnt any thingits almost impossible to make one literate, reason being they will neither be willing nor reluctant to learn. For those educated from here on you gain knowledge not you start learning. There is difference between gaining knowledge and learning knowledge. There is biological reason for it also.*

*Than why am I speaking of literacy ,here when I speak of literacy than I mean shedding their ignorance which will make them realize the importance of life. Through various community programme we can shed their ignorance and make them socially aware. When out of ignorance they will be able to know what is god and bad. At least they can distinguish between various life situation and analyze on it, this will increase knowledge. Knowledge does not merely lies in the text but it has origin from nature and even an illiterate can obtain knowledge certainly not those taught in universities, colleges and schools but those life lesson which every one learn from society and nature.*

*Awareness : Through various community programme they should be made to realize the importance of their life and curiosity and importance of future prospects of their children. They should have the feeling that I will not let my children live the life which I have been living. They should be made aware about social welfare and importance of society.*

*Self Dependency:- Preferably they should be trained to be self dependent. They should be provided skills to enhance their wages. Remember a skilled labour always performs better than unskilled and the skilled one will always produce better quality of product than the unskilled labour. Hence they should be provided proper skill so that can depend up on themselves.*

*Co-operative society:- Keeping the ability of their skills women should be encouraged to establish self help group or co-operative society. They can establish some*

*Financial support: Govt should provide financial support to such co-opertive society and self help group after satisfying their intent and willingness to run such group. This will create more job among them.*

*Labour reform: There should be a justified wages system for them and there should be a time fixed beyond which they should not be allowed to work. Since they have the responsibility to look after their children also.*

*Health consciousness:- Since report suggest that at certain work places were women works, it affects their health and consequentially the livelihood of their children. Women under poverty mostly living in the slums live in unhygienic condition. It has a major impact on their health and also their children.*

*Lack of awareness and resources regarding the food make their children malnourished, might be they have a feeling that from here on they might not bring a major change in their life but probably through health consciousness they can make their children future bright if they parent them wisely.*

*Life is precious and poverty should not defeat life,*

*perhaps life should defeat poverty. This is possible through a proper policy and rigorous implementation. If Governments around the world make this their priority certainly we will end poverty by 2030 which is United Nation Target.*

*Probably In India we might be able to do it well before that.*

*SushmaSwaraj , External affair Minister of India at UN General Assembly in 2017 ,had assured that India will do all that to achieve the UN goal of ending world Poverty by 2030. This is possible only when The Leaders around the world consider the poor as their own and not a democratic tool for a mere vote. Probably India will achieve the target before time.*

CHAPTER XI

# Child abuse and its protection

> *"O' son of kunti for all the species of life that are produced , the material nature is the womb and I am the seed- Giving father. Its I who impregnate them.*
> *-Lord Krishna(Bhagwat Gita 14;3) "*

*Vedic scriptures prophets to respect the life of every creatures and its filled with numerous example and Many Great Kings and Sages have practiced it. Unfortunately in today's world I see prominent world leaders fascination for Dogs , unfortunately they have overlooked the importance of those innocent children who are leading a miserable life deprived of the joy of childhood. Probably ,just because you all have underestimated their importance. A dog can live in palace and in the bedroom of prominent personalities but a human child is suffering on the streets and else where just out of seer ignorance of world leaders.*

*Before I begin on the topic in short let me narrate you a story, In India about 30 kilometers from my birth place. Some years back , A teacher picked up a shepherd, taught him, trained him and made him a king who ruled all over India. The shepherd Was King Chandragupta and the teacher was Chanakya. They both belong to my native district, champaran in Bihar.*

*Our scriptures prophets that love a child till the age of five from there on till 16 bring them up with discipline and from their on treat them as your friend. So childhood has been given utmost importance .it goes on to the extent of parenting achild in the mothers womb. So parenting should start right from the womb. Unfortunately the poor cant afford it and the leaders don't care it. For them what matters it a vote and in many country they have various means to lure them.*

*Any way*

*Child is that seed of them nation , which if nurtured well in a proper environment can become a tree which can give fruits to many for the generation to come, if not they become a liability indirectly for a nation. The govt. has to frame various policy for their livelihood if they are not capable of earning. Govts.should think instead of paying them later why not invest in their childhood so that they become a self dependent citizen and contribute in the nation Building.*

*Forms of child Abuse*

*Mortality:-Due to various reason many children die early in the childhood. They develop various type of disease mainly because of malnourishment and hence die early. Apart from this they have little resource and means to cure their child of from the disease they develop early in the childhood.*

*Trafficking:- Trafficking is one of the traumatic form of child abuse. Under this children's are kidnapped by various groups and armed forces for fulfilling their agenda. They treat them worst than animals and force them to do work of their need. In most of the country armed forces are involved in child trafficking. UNICEF has done commendable job in releasing them from out of their trap and restoring their life. I call it a traumatized because a child who should be enjoying his child with their parents is being deprived of parenting and their their life getting spoilt.*

*Child labour:- child labour is the most prevalent forms of child abuse. I have seen children below fourteen working late night at several highway motel. Wonder for them were is the human right sleeping?. A rapist is granted human right access but what about those children working late night and washing plates and cleaning the dinner table at those road side highway restaurants.*

*Being an spiritualist I travel frequently to the spiritual places all over India and have found children of tender age just standing in front of temple for putting sandal paste on your head merely for some money, that's nothing less than begging.*

*Frankly I consider both the concerned authority and the Govt. equally responsible this form of abuse.*

*Child marriage: In India mostly in the state of Rajasthan child marriage still prevails, since I am a frequent traveler to Rajasthan and perhaps one of the place I love the most in India, might be because of past life connection , they say sex ratio is less in Rajasthan that's why we go for child marriage. Our sages have advised to solemnized marriage only when you have completed you education, scientifically they are right, when we loose our sperm it hamper our memory, at a age when a children has just obtained the age of puberty there sexual inclination will be at all time high because of the hormonal changes occurring in the body, this will lead to excessive indulgence in sex which will hamper their strength memory and vigor. This has been clearly mentioned in the Vedic text. Therefore any form of child marriage even you belong to very rich family should be avoid unless you want your child memory to shrink in the tender age.*

*Marriage is all about shouldering responsibility, a child who cannot feed themselves how could he be able to feel his counterpart and if at all he obtains a progeny.*

*Sexual:- sexual abuse is more frequent in the poor children because of social and economic insecurity. Young girls are kidnapped and groomed for sexual pleasure. Due to lack of knowledge and protection they involve many forms of sex some time with some time without consent resulting in to early pregnancy.*

*Causes of Child abuse*

*Poverty: Poverty is the root cause of child abuse where out of compulsion to meet daily necessities such as food clothes and shelter children are forced to work. Many a time being compelled by their parents.*

*Illiteracy:- Since most of the children are illiterate due to lack of resources and willingness and a sinful parenting they don't see any option but to do menial jobs .*

*Sinful Parenting: In most of the cases their parents are also illiterate hence they live in ignorance and compel their children to do any sorts of job they can with whatever money they could earn.*

*Measures to protect Child abuse*

*Education:- A doubting soul perishes and ignorance is the root of doubt. Ignorance can be shed away through education and knowledge. Every child should be provided a compulsory primary education , attaining which if they have curiosity can rise further in the field of knowledge and education if not they can at least become self dependent and know the real purpose of life. Along with compulsory primary education they should be allowed to pursue their hobby during their primary education this hobby will later on turn out to be their skill, which trained in it they can become self dependent.*

*Malnutrition:- there should be proper policy by Govt. to abolish malnutrition, probably it should start from the womb of the mother. Most cases of child mortality are due to under nourishment of children in the womb, which result in to many type of diseases .Their brain does not get developed due to malnourishment and hence their memory levels are far below average to compete with the normal children. Even those living above the poverty line should be made aware of the importance of child care I the womb. Due to malnourishment many children become stunted.*

*Care in Pregnancy :- Women should be made aware of the importance of foetus care. It's a fact that about 80% of the brain get developed in the mother's womb and remaining 20% for rest of the life. So food in the pregnancy is of utmost importance and it should contain proper nutrients.*

*Stringent law:- There should be stringent law to abolish child labour and it should be implemented efficiently on the ground. Measure should be taken by govt. to prevent parents from forcing children in to child labour. There should be law to punish parents of the children who is propelling a child to do labour.*

*Its said child is the father of Nation. Today's children will be tomorrows performing citizens it all depends up on their upbringing. I live it up to the parents and Govts. Around the world either you invest them in their childhood and upbringing and make them a responsible and performing citizens or pay them for whole of their life. Option is up to you all.*

CHAPTER XII

# Farmers Distress in Emerging Economies

*"From yagya it rain ,and from rain the grains are produced.*

*_ Bhagwatgita"*

*Isn't the rain one of the sole reason for farmers distress around the world.*

*I don't find the exact word of yagya in any of the English dictionary, I beg pardon if it exists but probably to the extent I searched in on Google non of it matched the exact meaning of yagna. Probably they should induct this word in English language as it is and define it.*

*Yagya include fire obligation, mantra chanting, worshiping and Imparting knowledge.*

*In the modern science we question God probably if I write even 10 books to prove that the atheist won't believe and to the one who has faith in god mere 10 words are sufficient.*

*Scientifically it has been proved that the smoke erupting from the fire obligation purifies the air in the surroundings. Scientist now talk of vibes and chanting of mantra exhibits a good vibes and create a spiritual atmosphere where its performed, same about the obligation done through knowledge, it also creates a environment of good vibes .*

*In an research Done in AIIMS New Delhi onGayatri mantra it indeed had the affect on the intelligence of the patient, it exactly for what the matra has been prescribed in the Vedas.*

*Another research on Mahamritunjay mantra is on going in RML New Delhi and till now there has been positive response on the patient of the Mantra.*

*So scientifically its very essential, I wonder those spiritual people are mocked and called mad. Even Swami Vivekananda has admitted it that people call the spiritualist mad.*

*Now that science has proved the importance of vibes and affects of it on environment , the fire obligation clears the air and curb pollution in the air, shouldn't the spiritualist be respected and encouraged. Don't they indirectly play a major role in the prevalence of peace in the society.*

*I have mentioned all this in order to make you realize the importance of nature and environment which indirectly is one of the reason for their distress. They have lost the tolerance capability and are ending their life very quickly.*

*In an advice to king yudhistra of Indraprashta( Delhi) BhismPitamah had said a farmer should donate some portion of his produce to the needy because when they plough the soil many creatures die. This creatures has their own importance and they are responsible for the fertility of soil.*

*Now let's discuss the main reason of farmers distress in the Global economy*

*Climate change: Climate change has resulted in to unseasonal rain , drought . the distribution of rain now is unequally distributed through out the various countries. When I was pursuing my higher secondary in BokaroJharkhand I have observed that during the rainy season it used to rain heavily in the various sectors of Bokaro but Chas just 2 kilometers from there had no rain at all. When I researched a bit on it I found that in Chas which is not a planned city there are few number of trees, where as in sector 1 which is just 2 kilometers from Bokaro used to have good showers since it contain trees at equitable distance.*

*Hence trees play a major role in bringing rain. We have cut tree as such they were our enemies and now we are reaping the fruits of those cut trees.*

*Excessive dependency on plastics:-Excessive use of plastics has polluted the not only the air but also the soil. Though most part of my life I have lived in cities but since last 8 years I have extensively travelled and spent my life in village all throughout India and I have found that people broom the surrounding and collect it at one place and burn it. Forget about villages I have found it happening in New Delhi were people are deemed to be more aware.*

*To all those people who are scientist and policy makers what have you all done about this till date. Could you just imagine what repercussion would it be happening on the air in the surrounding where it burns. In the village particularly where I live I restrain them not to burn the plastic but the truth is such practice is prevalent. This is one of the main elements of air pollution, perhaps more severe than emissions of vehicles and factories. Carbon wastage of the industries does play role in air pollution, but that is visible and the govt can regulate that very easily, but how can you stop the plastics burning in the house hold.*

*So the two main reason behind climate change is*

*Cutting of trees and menace of plastics and plastic waste.*

*Yes! Carbon waste of industry does has its role in air pollution in climate change.*

*Replenishing fertility of soil:- Due to excessive use of insecticides , pesticides and chemical fertilizers the important creatures living in the soil are dying, hence the fertility of soil around the world is replenishing.*

*Lack of Intent by Their successor:- lack of intent in farming and profitability has led to their children not taking interest in farming. They are looking for some other option instead of farming which would fetch them more money. Probably they are not aware of the opportunities in farming.*

*Price:-Due to unfavorable and in competitive price they are losing their hope in farming.*

*Quality :- Due to degradation of fertility of soil and climate the quality of the soil has decreased, due to which they are not able to compete with the products in the international market that would generate more competitive price and opportunity for them.*

*Measures to end the farmers distress*

*Menace of plastics:- To Curb plastic menace there should be stringent law and should be implemented and executed truthfully. Substitute for plastic should be discovered as soon as we can, in the mean while we should curb the use of plastic as much as we can. Govt.should encourage and promote entrepreneurship in the field of plastic and waste management. There should be appropriate fund allocation probably a tie up with private institutes for finding substitute for plastics.*

*Organic Farming:- there should be extensive use of organic fertilizers .organic fertilizers have less chemicals and are not harmful for the creatures in the soil. It has been found in the research that it increases the productivity of grains, fruits and vegetables.*

*Planting Trees: Recently there indeed has been willingness from Govt. shown regarding tree plantation, that's a good sign; at least we have realized the importance of tree and plantation. But there doesn't end the journey, it should be the responsibility of the society where the saplings are planted to take care of it till it take the shape of a tree. And the Government should monitor. I think you all know the importance of tree so I need not to speak more on that. What many of you know about tree is that in Hindu scriptures tree are considered as a Guru (teacher). In associated with planets and one of the example I would like to mention here is Gular Tree is associated with Venus. Venus Governs semen in astrology and scientifically it has been proven that eating gular with sweet increases the sperm count you all love science, so see how scientific the Vedic scripture is. Therefore plant as much tree as you all can it will help in cleaning air, bringing the temperature down and bring rain.*

*Scientific farming: Generally in India were farmers are mostly illiterate though not ignorant, need to be taught about scientific farming. Since there has been change in the fertility of the soil due to undistributed rain and change in climate, they need to be taught about crop which would be best suited for according to their soil in their field.*

*To those who are involved in seed research and hybridization, do keep in to your mind about the quality of soil and climate before hybridizing any seed. Productivity of a particular seed depends up the climate most. Yes the quality of seed do matter but than climate has a major role to play right from sprouting to bearing the ingredients. if we produce a quality seed the quality of seed will increase making the produce more competitive and fetching them a better price.*

*Probably the farmers even in the village are aware of modern farmingequipments and I live up on their marketing team to advertise about the modern farming equipments that would better than the Govt. doing that.*

*Competitive market: Farmers should be made aware of digital market where they can directly sell the produce and fetch a competitive price. Govt of India has developed a Appnamed eNAM where farmers can selltheir agriculture produce .*

*Quality: Quality of produce can be bettered by soil testing ,knowing the deficiency and fulfilling that very ingredients in the soil through fertilizers. Fertilizers should not contain chemicals which kills the required creatures in the soil.*

*Export: By increase in the quality of seed their chance of export will increase .manyGovt around the world has stringent quality test, and for that a product to pass the quality has to improved. Govt.can assist in export, by providing financial and consulting support, Educate a farmer but the improvement of quality depends up on fertility and it lies with the farmers .*

*Crop Insurance: Due to - Ways to double Income:*

1. *Increasing the fertility of the soil*
2. *Appropriate crop for appropriate soil*
3. *Scientific Knowledge of Farming*
4. *Adding value of to the Raw Product*
5. *Increasing the quality Of seed/Use of Quality seed*
6. *Competitive price*

*God gave us life to live , perform some action for the man kind ,but we have been lost in to the analysis of financial statements and are always lost in the assets and liabilities of balance sheet . we have forgotten to respect the Nature. We are busy in quantifying and multiplying our wealth and have no sense of responsibility about our future generation. To the corporate who call yourself rich if you think you all , will and can make your children knowledgeable and wealthy by teaching them at Harvard and oxford than to you all I don't think that you all have accomplished your responsibility ,just tell me will your children will you children eat dollar, pounds ,euro , rupee, bronze or silver, where will they breathe ? on Saturn? I mentioned Saturn because you all say its made up of gas.*

*If so store it in the Reserve bank of your country, might be after you they will have cents, pounds and paise at breakfast, dollar, rupee and euro in lunch and gold silver and bronze at dinner before going to bed.*

*If not wake up, your childrens have to breathe the same air which the poor will, probably when it rain it will not be merely on your roof top because you are a billionaire. Groom your children in to a responsible human being. Teach them about the importance of Nature. Two world Leaders have been awarded the prize for their contribution in protection of environment ,Narendramodi and EmmanuelMacron.I wish USA think again on Paris agreement. For your children to live happily the environment and the nature need to be protected and Respected.*

CHAPTER XIII

# Germany ;Budget surplus and its effective utilization

*Following eight are in themselves a source of joy in this world and indicates that people are happy*

1. *Social gatherings and interaction of friends*
2. *Increase in wealth*
3. *Affection between sons and fathers*
4. *Fondness of the couples for sex*
5. *Use of appropriate ,pleasant and timely words in conversation*
6. *Raise in status among equals*
7. *Acquisition of desired goals and social approval*
8. *Appreciation in congragations*

*-Vidur*

*Govt. business is to do no business*

- *AtalbihariBajpai ( Former Prime minister Of India)*
- *I read in reputed journal that some economist have advise German Govt. to invest that money for business activities.*
- *I ask you one question which is best source to invest, the human resource that once made successful will pay you taxes for whole of your life , forget tax for a moment, if they become a responsible citizen will indirectly contribute in nation building by becoming a responsible citizen, a responsible father, brother , friend, mother,sister,wife or some few millions or billions of*

*interest earned ? Decide it, after all you all are experienced economist! Which will contribute to the nation more, those interest or a knowledgeable citizen.*

*Germany is a Developed country and German technology are famous worldwide. Probably there are enough of economist sitting around there to debate on demand , supply and exports etc.. etc.. perhaps we have enough time to discuss on that and probably will do later*

*In this article my sole focus will be on the optimum utilization of the budget surplus.*

*The Govt. should invest the budget surplus in solving the current and expected future social and economic problems.*

Social problems

**Family problems:**-*At current Germany is battling with family problems, that has hampered the social harmony in the family. This has led to increase in mental problem such as depression. Data says the about 16 percent of people are suffering from depression.*

*You know , in a family if the father and mother fight in front of teenager, it has affect on the mind of the teenager, like wise such battle at home has lead to social disharmony in the society*

**Marriage problems:**-*This social disharmony has lead to increase in the divorce case , subsequently childrens are suffering from this menace. They are not able to get a responsible parenting.*

**Child Care:**- *Due to divorce case the fight between the parents for their right has led to step motherly treatment. There is probably no care about them. For the couple probably a new partner has become more important than the children they have produced. Probably they are or have become unaware of the institution of marriage.*

***Aging problems:-****Germany is currently facing aging problems and the current average age their citizen is around 44.*

Economic problems:-

*Recently here has been fall in the consumer spending leading to fall in demand, although to some extent its because of global trade war.*

*There has been fall in the manufacturing index.*

***Bureaucratic problems:-****over all the German bureaucracy is good and has good bureaucrats', probably they need some innovation in the bureaucratic human resource and process.*

*looking at the above problems German Govt. should invest the surplus in following areas*

*family welfare: The Govt. should invest in infrastructure in community development programmes ,like community centre consisting of recreation centre, entertainment and counseling for married and future couple for bringing awareness in the institution of marriage, sex and importance of children in life.*

*Child welfare: children should be taught the benefits and ways of using social media websites. This is one of the reasons for their getting depressed, because they compare with their counterparts. Childrens have turned violent which is not a good sign for the society*

*Education :- there should be reform in the primary education to make them mentally strong to be prepared to face the future challenges. There should be right blend of practical and theoretical education with adequate recreation at the primary level. They should be provided holistic approach in their upbringing. Policy should be framed and implemented and the required budget should be allocated for the said policy.*

*Research in management: setting up infrastructure in the field of business management research. This will bring reforms in the managerial capacity and bureaucratic management process and Business leaders.*

*Research in green motor vehicle: Germany is known for its technology in the motor vehicles, Govt should raise infrastructure in the area of green vehicle , solar vehicle, vehicle being run on hydrogen etc..this will help them retain their dominance in the motor vehicle segment in the world.*

*Parliamentary and Bureaucratic reform:- The Govt. can set up infrastructure for skilling , educating and training for bureaucratic human resources. This will let them induct quality human resources in the Govt. institution who will efficiently execute and implement the Govt. Policies.*

*Solving the aging Problems:- They should set up infrastructure of research in the field of increasing fertility in men and women; To the extent I know excessive use of opiods is one of the reason for decrease in the fertility. There are other factors too. Stress also contribute to infertility.*

*Healthcare reforms:- Since Germany is battling with aging problems they will have to face with problems related to elderly people and such sectors requires invest and research about the future prospects of the health of the elderly citizens.*

*Recreation :- To me depression is not a disease rather a thought process and a belief that one has lost the battle of life. Its just because their self esteem has fallen down. So investment in the recreation segment will not only improve the happiness level of the citizen but also increase the tourism of the country.*

*Social cost and benefits will always supersedes monetary benefits for a Govt. and therefore the Govt. around the world should focus on every means they can bring to prevail harmony and welfare in the society. If Germany invest their surplus in the above area certainly their future generation will reap the benefits from it.*

CHAPTER XIV

# Desire; An Spiritual Analysis

> *"Desire is the Root of all Evil ,Hope Kills perseverance "*

*In Astrology desire is considered as an obstacle in life, just because it never ends. So long as we keep on desiring, our life doesn't get relinquished, we remain entangled in to the day to day worldly affairs of life .There might be fulfillment to our wants but never to our desires.*

*It's said in shreemadbhagwatam that covetousness is an incurable disease. To much extent it's the Attitude of covetousness that we keep on desiring and chasing all throughout our life to fulfill our desire. when our desired doesn't get fulfilled we get stuck in our life. Hence its termed as a obstacle.*

*The question here arises what about the corporate , they have their monetary goals and they are always in the process to fulfill that desire. Is that aobstacle ? Everyone has a life goal and probably every personal goal some what constitute of desire. And life without a goal is a life wasted. We need to have a goal in life and a desire to fulfill that goal has nothing wrong in it.*

*In Sanskrit entrepreneurship has been given the term udhamita that originates from the word udhammeans efforts . Rig veda says that o human at the first part of your life gain knowledge and than from that knowledge through purusarth earn your livelihood.*

*From both the verse , we derive that so long as our worldly achievements are obtained through udham and purusarth our desires neither corrupts nor entangled us, but soon as we adopt various other means to fulfill our desires we get entangled in to it.*

*In BhagwatGeeta desire has been considered as one of our enemy.*

*The reason why I am writing on this topic is just to make you all aware about the repercussion of non fulfillment of desire. Desire when fulfilled motives you and bring you in a state of joy and happiness on the contrary when not fulfilled you start loosing your self esteem and deviating from the path you have laid from your self. In that case the same desire acts as your enemy because it lays you off from your path and you get lost in to the world. There the state of depression starts. Depression is nothing but non fulfillment of our desires.*

*Entrepreneurship is all about udham()and that should be the only means to fulfill every entrepreneurial goal. when purusarth is the medium to achieve our worldly goal we neither blame others nor to our self on the non fulfillment of our desires, rather accept it as Gods will and move on to our next goal of life.*

*In this world we cannot remain idle without performing Action.. Nature will propel us to perform action based up on the three primordial nature of human. We are bounded by those qualities depending upon the modes of nature. And that constitute our desire. Since every one performs action all has a desire and they find their own suitable way to fulfill their desire. A person with no desire is an ascetic.*

*You might be thinking that can an ascetic be an entrepreneur, Yes ! he can if he has no desire for himself and performs action on the will of god by surrendering before him and giving up the fruits of action . in that state any one can be called as a ascetic.*

*But don't worry! I am not telling you to be ascetic; nor will I, the reason being so long you don't extinguish your desire you won't be liberated and the best way to be liberated is to fulfill all your desires; and our scriptures permits us to fulfill all our desires because without their fulfillment we have to take birth again and again. The ultimate goal of a human is to attain salvation and that's when all our desire get extinguished and our desire will get extinguished only when we have achieved and enjoyed it.*

*Take some time, write down your desire, have a plan and go for it, might be you dream to be a millionaire a billionaire, a politician, actor or what so ever it be, just fulfill all your worldly desire nothing wrong with it.*

*Perhaps everyone on this earth are born with a motive and that get performed by action, depending up on the qualities we posses .qualities depend up on our attitude and attitude depends up on three modes of nature and three modes of our nature depends up on the action performed in our previous birth.*

*So while fulfilling your desire always bear it in to your mind that if you adopt illegal and unethical path to fulfill your desire , you incur sin and probably you will have a next birth and you have to reap the fruits of those action either in this birth or the next. and that will keep on going till you extinguish or fulfill all your desire. Your desire has direct connection with your action and always check the motive of your action because that's what propels our desire.*

*Desire directly has connection with our action. So our Action has to be truthful and honest or else our desire will be evil, an evil desire might land you in hell if not jail.*

*Some one asked me that in bhagwatgeeta Krishna says that its I who propels every one through illusion to performs action!*

*Don't live in a fool paradigm and waste all your life that its god who is propelling you to perform evils! Its you nature that is propelling you to do your action and not god. Change your nature in return that will change your quality and finally action. If it was God who was doing all that Than why have you taken birth. God might do everything what the use of human on this earth?*

*So take all this scraps out of your mind and make a plan to fulfill all your desire through udham and purusarth. Remember what exactly god says in Geeta is that I propel every one to perform action based up on his Nature. Its all your Nature change your nature and everything will change if not all through out your life you will keep on blaming Krishna that its he who is doing everything.*

9 798885 030878

Printed by Libri Plureos GmbH in Hamburg,
Germany